Introduction to Computing

Eric Frick

Published by Eric Frick 2021

Last Update February, 2022

Copyright

Foreword

Hello, and welcome to the exciting world of cloud computing. I specifically designed this book to be the companion book to the video course that I have hosted on my website. You might think of this as the lab manual for the course. You can get more out of this book by reviewing the accompanying videos in the web-based course.

You have free access to this course by purchasing this book. I included the link to this course in the introduction section of this book. Thank you for purchasing this book, and welcome to the class!

Contents

Chapter 1 Introduction

Hello and welcome to the world of cloud computing! I put this book together for people who are looking to get started with cloud computing and want to know why it is such a hot topic. I assume you are a complete beginner and will take you through step by step to get you going. In this chapter, I will describe the structure of this book and some supporting resources I have provided that will give you some more options for learning this material. So let's get started!

1.1 Welcome

Hello, and welcome to the book! This book is the first part of a series that is an introduction to cloud computing concepts. I have based these books on courses that I have taught online to entry-level students on various web platforms. I designed this course to give you some of the theory behind cloud systems and some practical experience using a real cloud system, like Amazon AWS.

I assume for this book and course that you are a complete beginner and have no previous experience with cloud computing. You will need a computer with a web browser to view the videos and access Amazon AWS. Also, you will need a valid credit card to sign up for your trial Amazon AWS account. Amazon will not charge you for the use of this account, but they require this for registration.

I wrote this book for absolute beginners and kept the materials to a reasonable length, so you could quickly get up to speed with cloud computing and see if this interests you for study further. I also wanted to mix in some of the theory and definitions of cloud computing, along with some practical, hands-on exercises, so you can not only read about systems, but actually learn to use them in practice.

1.2 Content Overview

In chapter 2 of this book, I will present core cloud concepts. These concepts include a base definition of cloud computing, and some key characteristics of cloud-based systems. Having a good grasp of these fundamentals will give you a firm foundation where you can build further knowledge of the services and features of public cloud providers.

Next, in chapter 3, we will glance at the state of the market for cloud-based systems. We will look at the current list of top cloud providers and the growth of the cloud computing market.

Finally, in chapter 4, we will look at the details of Amazon AWS, which is the leading cloud provider in the market today. I will start this section with an overview of Amazon AWS and the services it offers.

Next, I will show you, step by step, how to sign up for a free trial AWS account. Once you have your account, we will look at the following key AWS services:

- AWS EC2 (Elastic Cloud Compute)
- AWS S3 (Simple Storage Service)
- AWS Lambda (Serverless Functions)

By the end of this book, you will understand key cloud concepts and have some hands-on experience with Amazon AWS.

1.3 Supporting Material

By purchasing this book, you will also receive free access to the video version of this class on my website. You can access this class by using the following link:

https://www.destinlearning.com/p/introduction-to-cloud-computing/?product_id=3360851&coupon_code=INTRO2021

If you have any difficulties signing up, please contact me at sales@destinlearning.com and I will send you a coupon code.

Thank you again for purchasing this book. If you have any feedback, please contact me. I want to make this book and course the very best they can be. With that in mind, let's get started on the material!

Chapter 2 Cloud Concepts

In this chapter, I will cover some of the fundamental concepts of cloud computing. These concepts are core to cloud computing systems and are common no matter which cloud provider you are using. We will first look at the definition of cloud computing and what differentiates cloud systems from traditional computing systems. Following that, we will look at a brief history of cloud computing and some of the underlying developments that allowed for the creation of today's public cloud systems. Next, we will look at the fundamental advantages and limitations of cloud computing. Finally, we will round out the discussion with a presentation of cloud service models.

2.1 What is Cloud Computing?

Cloud computing delivers computing services to remote users over a network. Private clouds are services that are intended to be utilized by a single organization. Both private or public networks can deliver these services. Public clouds provide computing services over the Internet and are generally available to anyone with a credit card. Public cloud service providers deliver these services via massively shared data centers. These shared data centers allow cloud service providers the ability to offer services that smaller, private companies could not afford to build in their own data centers. Pictured above is one of Microsoft's Azure data centers.

Cloud computing has its roots in some of the early mainframe services offered to customers in the pre-2000 era. Many early services provided a paid service that users could consume remotely. However, network infrastructures, during that era, limited the number and services that the infrastructure could provide to remote users. Salesforce.com was one of the early pioneers of Software as a Service (SAAS) in 1999. These types of services enabled many companies to implement CRM (Customer Relationship Management) systems quickly.

Amazon launched some new services called, Infrastructure as a Service (IAAS), in 2006. They have since followed up with a large number of cloud services. Microsoft Azure began its cloud services in 2010. Since then, the leading IT companies now have their own cloud service offerings. The following diagram predicts that the cloud computing market is projected to reach $127 billion by 2017. Figure 3, from Forbes, describes the dramatic growth of cloud-based systems by different areas. I will define these areas later in this chapter.

Figure 3 Forecast: Global Public Cloud Market Size, 2011 To 2020

The spreadsheet detailing this forecast is available online.

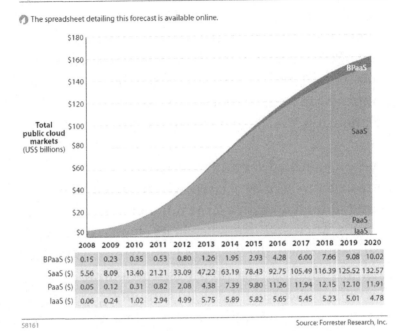

	2008	2009	2010	2011	2012	2013	2014	2015	2016	2017	2018	2019	2020
BPaaS ($)	0.15	0.23	0.35	0.53	0.80	1.26	1.95	2.93	4.28	6.00	7.66	9.08	10.02
SaaS ($)	5.56	8.09	13.40	21.21	33.09	47.22	63.19	78.43	92.75	105.49	116.39	125.52	132.57
PaaS ($)	0.05	0.12	0.31	0.82	2.08	4.38	7.39	9.80	11.26	11.94	12.15	12.10	11.91
IaaS ($)	0.06	0.24	1.02	2.94	4.99	5.75	5.89	5.82	5.65	5.45	5.23	5.01	4.78

58161   Source: Forrester Research, Inc.

Figure 3 Global Public Cloud Market Size 2011 to 2020

(http://www.forbes.com/sites/louiscolumbus/2015/01/24/roundup-of-cloud-computing-forecasts-and-market-estimates-2015/#41cd412c740c)

2.2 The History of Cloud Computing

1960's	Packet Switching
1970's	ARPANET
1980's	TCP/IP
1990's	World Wide Web
2000-2010	Amazon AWS
2011-2021	Micosoft Azure + Google Cloud

In this section, I will describe a brief history of cloud computing. I will focus on some of the key technologies that pre-dated cloud computing, but provided the key components that cloud computing depends on today in order to operate.

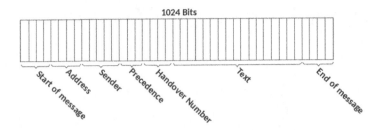

Packet Switching

In the early 1960s, several groups researched packet switching as a way to allow computers to communicate with each other. Until that time, circuit switching had been the prefered method for computer communications. Through the work of several research groups at MIT, the Rand Institute, and the National Physical Laboratory in England, they developed some of the basic concepts that the Internet uses today.

The block message, pictured above, was suggested by Paul Baran in 1964, and published during his initial research on packet switching. This concept was later referred to as a packet and was incorporated in the initial designs of the ARPANET. This design was a radical departure from using dedicated circuits and expensive hardware. At the time, this concept was met with a large amount of scepticism from the engineering community.

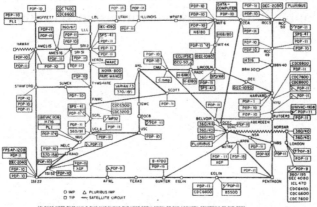

ARPANET

In the late 1970s, work that was sponsored by the Defense Advanced Research Project Agency, or DARPA, developed a network of computers called ARPANET. (Advanced Research Projects Agency NETwork) This effort developed a method for different computers to communicate with each other. This research included computers from both military installations and research universities. In the early 1980s, the project grew from an initial handful of machines, to hundreds. The structure and growth of the ARPANET provided the basic model for our current Internet.

Pictured above is a map of the ARPANET computers from March 1977. At that time, this was a state-of-the-

art network, and it was growing rapidly. The
ARPANET continued to be used for research and
development until it was decommissioned in 1990.

TCP/IP

The underlying protocol the Internet uses today, for network traffic, is called TCP/IP. It stands for Transmission Control Protocol/Internet Protocol. While working for the Defense Advanced Research Project Agency, two scientists, Vint Cerf and Bob Kahn, developed TCP/IP. They migrated the ARPA network to this protocol and eventually migrated the entire system in 1983. TCP/IP eventually became the standard for all military networks. Following this success, they published their work in the Request for Comments (RFC) standards. This allowed TCP/IP to move into the public domain. This work provided the basis for the networking standards we still use today.

The figure displayed below is the basic architecture of TCP/IP. It is a layered architecture, which allows for the flexibility of this protocol. The design of this protocol has been so successful that it has been in widespread use on the Internet since the 1990s.

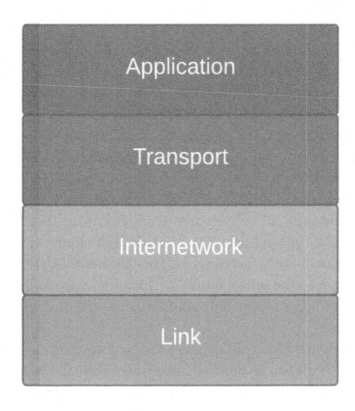

World Wide Web (WWW)

Tim Berners-Lee, (pictured above) who worked at CERN, the European Organization for Nuclear Research, invented the World Wide Web, or WWW, in the 1989-1990 time frame. CERN and Tim Berners-Lee developed the first web server. This was driven by the need for researchers around the world to share information. After the first web server was developed,

CERN published instructions on how other institutions could set up their own web servers. These instructions resulted in several hundred other institutions hosting their own web servers. In 1993, CERN opened the code, for the web servers and the browser, to the public domain, making the software freely available. Once the software was in the public domain, it provided the basis for the explosive growth of the World Wide Web, followed by the Internet.

Amazon Web Services is Launched

In 2006, Amazon launched Amazon Web Services. This service was a unique and innovative offering for the marketplace at the time. Amazon initially offered two key services:

- Amazon S3 - Simple Storage Service
- Amazon EC2 - Elastic Cloud Compute

These are still two key services on the platform today. We will cover these services in more detail later in the book. Amazon has consistently added more and more services since the initial launch, and today offers hundreds of cloud services.

In 2010, Amazon migrated all of its internal operations to AWS, and then began to concentrate on growing their business. Since they were first in the market, Amazon has had a consistent, large lead in the market. Over time though, Microsoft has been aggressively growing their cloud business and is threatening to overtake AWS for the lead.

Competitors Enter the Space

Soon after the launch of AWS, several large competitors entered the scene. In 2010, Microsoft launched Windows Azure and began to educate their existing customers about the advantages of cloud-based systems. In 2014, Microsoft renamed the service to Microsoft Azure. Since that time, they have been investing heavily in this offering and are a close, second place competitor to AWS. Many analysts believe that Microsoft, at some point, will become the number one cloud service.

Google launched their first cloud offering in 2011. The first service they offered was their App Engine service. Currently, they are in third place, in terms of market share, behind Amazon and Microsoft.

2.3 What Are the Advantages of Cloud Computing?

In this section, I will describe some of the key advantages of cloud computing, and why it is an attractive alternative for hosting major software projects, for many companies. I will outline the advantages in four key areas.

Utility Computing

Cloud computing offers a utility model for computing. You only pay for the resources you use, much like your power company. For example, if you have a server running in the cloud, you will probably be charged by the minute. If you do not need the resource 24/7, you can turn it off when you are not using it, and you will not incur charges.

You will, however, pay for the storage costs. These costs, though, are generally small, compared to runtime services.

Dynamic Scaling

Most cloud systems also provide a model where you can quickly scale up your computing needs, to meet a dynamic demand. This model is a much more cost-effective way to meet the demands of systems with very dynamic usage patterns.

An example of this is a tax filing system with peak demands around filing times. The system can be set up to automatically add more resources as the load increases, and then scale back resources when the load decreases. This feature can be a huge advantage for developers, since it is easy to access and rarely requires specific coding to take advantage of these services.

Another advantage of cloud computing systems is they generally offer self-provisioning models, where end users can provision servers and network resources quickly. Usually, new servers can be built and brought online in a matter of minutes. In the physical server world, this can take weeks, or even months. This time savings can be a significant advantage to developers, who might need to get new code to market quickly.

Disaster Recovery

Another benefit of most cloud systems is that they offer advanced services for failover and disaster recovery. These generally involve add-on fees, but they allow companies to consume these services quickly. Many smaller companies cannot afford to build an alternate data center for redundancy.

Standards Compliance

One more advantage of cloud computing is that many providers need to comply with many industry standard certifications, such as HIPAA and PCI. These certifications are very expensive for smaller companies to achieve on their own.

2.4 The Limitations of Cloud Computing

Physical Access

One major limitation of this technology is that you do not have physical access to your data and the servers you have provisioned. Many companies and government organizations require their employees to have access to these physical environments. This requirement is simply impossible with the cloud computing model.

If you have systems that have these requirements, you must deploy them on servers that your employees can access. Another limitation is that often, you do not control the network resources to connect to the cloud system. If there is a problem with that network, you will not be able to physically access the network resources, which are in your cloud service provider's data center. Even if your systems are running, they are no good to anyone if you cannot connect to them over a network.

Security Concerns

Another concern, for most companies and government agencies, is that a third party provides security for these systems. You do not have direct control. This situation makes many companies nervous enough not to adopt these systems. By putting provisions in the service providers contract, to enact penalties in cases of service failure, you can mitigate some of these risks.

Also, many companies are now adopting a hybrid model, where some resources reside in an on-premises data center, and the remainder live in the cloud. In this way, they can pick the environment that best suits their requirements.

2.5 Cloud Service Models

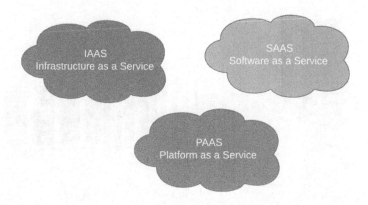

There are three major cloud computing service models:

- Infrastructure as a Service (IaaS)
- Platform as a Service (PaaS)
- Software as a Service (SaaS)

I will now describe each one of these in more detail.

Infrastructure as a Service

Infrastructure as a Service, or IaaS, is a way to provide virtualized resources over the Internet. This model supports rapid provisioning of servers, routers, network resources, and anything to build your own, complete data center in the cloud. Also, many systems provide scripting languages and other resources. So, much of this work can be automated. This capability allows companies to cut down on the labor required to maintain their server infrastructure. These systems also provide advanced services, such as dynamic scaling.

A good example of Infrastructure as a Service is the Google Cloud Platform's Compute Engine service. The Compute Engine service allows users to quickly provision servers in the cloud, and they are billed by the actual amount of usage. Google bills out their servers on per-second usage. If you turn the server off, you will not be billed for runtime services. But you will still be charged for the storage cost of the virtual hard disk. The storage cost is very cheap, compared to the runtime cost. Other cloud providers, such as Microsoft and Amazon, offer similar services.

You can read more about the Google Compute Engine service here:
https://cloud.google.com/compute/

Platform as a Service

Platform as a Service, or PaaS, allows customers to build and deploy applications, without the complexity of building physical infrastructure and configuring software. For example, Microsoft Azure offers Microsoft SQL server databases as a service. With this database service, you do not need to build servers or install software. You only need to load your database and tables into this system. However, with most types of services, a rework is often required. Many companies look at these services when building a *new* system or performing *significant* upgrades to older systems.

Software as a Service

Software as a Service, or SaaS, allows an organization to consume entire hosted applications over the Internet or private network. With this model, there is no software to install or maintain, since the vendor takes complete responsibility for this. There are many examples of this model on the market today. Office 365, from Microsoft, fits in this model. Although you can install Office locally on your computer, there are also cloud-based versions of the product, which allow you to run Office in a browser. Also, users can store data in the cloud on Microsoft OneDrive, and email can be stored in the cloud as well. Other examples of SaaS vendors include NetSuite, a major ERP vendor, and Service Now, which is a cloud-based service and ticketing system for IT shops.

2.6 The Economics of Cloud Computing

One of the major considerations that is fueling the explosive growth of cloud computing is the economic advantages of migrating on premise services to the cloud. Cloud-based systems are cheaper from a startup standpoint and allow teams to field systems more rapidly. Let's look at a simple example and the details from a cost and time to market perspective. In this scenario, the equipment that is needed is a 64 Gigabyte server with a 1 terabyte hard drive. I did not include any other equipment such as networking gear etc. to keep the example simple.

In this example, I got pricing data from a traditional equipment provider, Dell Inc. and data from the AWS cost calculator online to compare what it would cost to buy a physical server and then to provide an equivalent server online. The table below presents the summary information of what I found.

Dell Server vs AWS EC2 Server

Initial Purchase

On Premise	Cost	Cloud (AWS Ohio	Cost
PowerEdge R740x Server	$9,465.37	x2gd.xlarge	$0.0(
64 GB Memory			
1TB Sata Drive			

Shipping Time	Dell Server	E2c Machine
		Less than 30 minu
	30 Days (from ᵛ	provision

Operating Cost (N	Dell Server	AWS Serv⸱
	$833.33	$252 ₃

Initial Purchase

For the initial purchase of the physical server, I went to the Dell web page and configured a daily middle of the road server and configured it with a 1TB SATA drive and 64 Gb of RAM. The purchase price of this server is $9,465.37. Compared to configuring an equivalent server in AWS, there is a $0 startup cost.

You simply need to have an account with AWS and then configure and launch the server. You will then pay for the server by the hour that you use it. With one server, this cost might not make an enormous difference to a large corporation, but it would make a significant difference for a project that requires 50 or 100 servers.

Shipping Time

When I configured the server on the Dell website, it listed an approximate 30 day time from order to delivery. Based on my experience in ordering hardware, this is a typical turnaround time for a server manufacturer. In contrast, there is no shipping time for the cloud-based solution at AWS. You simply need to configure the server and it will be up and running in just a few minutes. This is an enormous advantage of cloud-based deployments: you can provision resources almost instantly. When a company is in a highly competitive environment, this time savings can represent a huge competitive advantage.

Operating Cost

Calculating the ongoing operating cost is difficult since it depends on the environment that the equipment is operating in. As an example, I assumed for the on-premise machine that the company spends $ one million annually supporting a data center of 100 machines. I then allocated a proportional monthly cost to this server, which came out to $833.33 per month to support this server. For the cost for the AWS server, I quoted the monthly cost from the AWS cost calculator to run this server in the Ohio region. Even if my on-premise calculations are way off, you can see from this example how affordable the cloud solution is compared to operating your own data center.

Summary

Although this is a very simple example, you can see the significant advantages that cloud computing offers in terms of purchase cost, time to market and ongoing operating expenses.

2.7 Cloud Concepts Quiz

1. Which company is the leading cloud computing vendor in the cloud market today?
    A. Microsoft
    B. Oracle
    C. Amazon
    D. IBM

2. What is one of the primary benefits of SaaS?
    A. You are free to modify the software as needed
    B. You can choose the version of the software you would like to use
    C. The system is an end-to-end solutions that the vendor maintains for you
    D. None of the above

3. What is IaaS?
    A. Internet Awareness Service
    B. Infrastructure as a Service
    C. Intelligent Advertising Agent Service

4. What is Amazon's cloud system called?
    A. Amazon AWS
    B. The Amazon Cloud System
    C. The Amazon Personal Cloud

5. Office 365 is an example of?
   A. IaaS
   B. PaaS
   C. SaaS
   D. None of the above

6. Having direct physical access to servers is an advantage to cloud computing.
   A. True
   B. False

7. Paying for only the cloud services and resources you are actually using is referred to as?
   A. Pay as You Go
   B. Utility Computing
   C. All of the above

8. The ability to easily scale systems up and down easily is referred to as?
   A. Autogen
   B. Elasticity
   C. Utility computing
   D. None of the above

9. The following are advantages of cloud computing?
   A. You can quickly provision resources
   B. You only pay for what you use
   C. Your systems are highly available
   D. All of the above

Chapter 3 The Cloud Market

In this section, I will describe the top ten cloud computing vendors for 2016. This list will continue to change over time, but it will give you an idea of the top companies that are involved. While the demand for cloud computing continues to rise, companies are responding to the demand with new and innovative services. Datamation has published their top ten cloud computing vendors for 2016.

Rank	Vendor
1	Amazon AWS
2	Microsoft Azure
3	IBM
4	Google Cloud Platform
5	Salesforce.com
6	Adobe
7	Oracle Cloud
8	SAP
9	Rackspace
10	Workday

Not surprisingly, Amazon is on top of the list. Many others on the list, though, are investing heavily and marketing their services aggressively to companies and government agencies. Many companies offer special, government-only cloud services to help secure federal, state, and local government contracts.

Some companies started with more traditional software and hardware models, but have now branched out into cloud computing. Salesforce.com makes almost all of its revenue from cloud services, and has been enjoying double-digit growth over the last few years.

In the early days of cloud computing, many companies were mostly interested in IaaS or platform offerings from companies like Amazon, Microsoft, Rackspace, or Google, but more SaaS-based offerings from companies such as Sales*force*.com, SAP, and Workday, have now seen tremendous growth. Also, many companies are now turning to platforms such as Sales*force*.com as an application development platform, opening up further opportunities for software developers.

The market for cloud computing products and services continues to grow and evolve quickly. The companies on this list are investing heavily in new products and services and are working hard to move up the list. Microsoft alone is spending billions annually in constructing new data centers for Azure. With this competition, the cost of cloud services will continue to drop and will further increase adoption.

Chapter 4 Amazon AWS

In this chapter, we will look in more detail at Amazon AWS, which is the leading cloud computing provider in the market today. We will start off looking at a brief history of AWS to give you some context of how they got to the position they are in today. Next, I will show you how to sign up for a free trial account with AWS. After you have your account, I will then show you how to use two of their most popular services, Elastic Cloud Compute (EC2) and Simple Storage Service (S3)

4.1 Amazon AWS Overview

So, what are Amazon Web services? Amazon Web services' cloud computing services are delivered by a large number of data centers, which Amazon has built on a worldwide basis. Amazon offers these services to both commercial and government customers, and is the leading cloud computing vendor in the market today.

Amazon AWS provides regional data centers on various continents across the globe. These regional data centers are further subdivided into availability zones. By providing these regional data centers and availability zones, Amazon can provide customers with multiple failover options, and also locate services closer to their customers.

If we look at a brief history of Amazon Web Services, (AWS) it was launched in 2008. In 2010, following the launch of Amazon Web Services, Amazon moved all of its operations to AWS, in order to run its own internal business. In 2010, Amazon also launched a certification program, for both developers and engineers, to operate Amazon cloud-based data centers. In 2013, Amazon was awarded the FedRAMP certification and began doing business with the US federal government. Until recently, Amazon did not report AWS income separately from the rest of the company's operations, but in 2015, they reported Q1 revenues of $1.57 billion for AWS.

Since 2008, Amazon has landed some high-profile customers. Two customers that run their large-scale web businesses on Amazon's infrastructure are Netflix and Expedia. Amazon also has such customers as Spotify, Comcast, and Coursera. If you look at their website, it will give you a more complete list of their current customers.

Services Offered

Amazon
S3

AWS
Lambda

Amazon Lightsail

Amazon
EC2

AWS Elastic
Beanstalk

Amazon Cognito

Amazon AWS offers a wide range of cloud computing services. This list of services is growing, and new services are released frequently. Computer services, storage, content delivery, database services, networking, and analytics are some of the services offered by Amazon AWS. Besides these services, AWS also offers enterprise applications, as well as mobile services, the Internet of Things, developer tools, and management tools.

Regional Coverage

The figure above is a listing of Amazon's regional coverage. These regions provide worldwide coverage, so you can locate computing resources closer to your customers in order to provide better performance. Each region is broken down into multiple availability zones to provide redundancy for each region. With all of these resources, Amazon AWS can provide worldwide coverage!

Currently, there are 24 launched regions, each with multiple availability zones. There are also more on the way!

In the next section, I will be demonstrating how to sign up for an account with Amazon, and also detail its free tier usage. Following that, I will show you how to log into the management console in Amazon AWS, and create a virtual machine.

In summary, Amazon offers services for Infrastructure as a Service, Platform as a Service, and Software as a Service. We have seen that the service list is very comprehensive. Also, Amazon is the leading cloud service provider in the market today, with many high-profile customers.

4.2 Amazon AWS Free Account

This section describes how to sign up for a free Amazon AWS account. Once you sign up, you can then use their cloud services from the web console.

Navigate to the AWS Web Page

First, go to http://aws.amazon.com/free in your web browser.

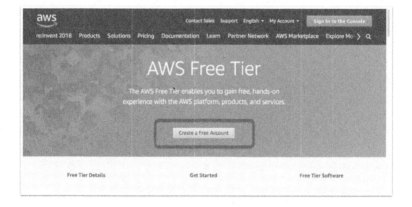

Read about the FREE tier

Next, read about the features of Amazon's free service tier. This trial lasts for 12-months. It does have limitations on the number of computer hours you can consume and the size of the virtual servers you can provision. These free services change from time to time, so scroll through the list to see the complete details.

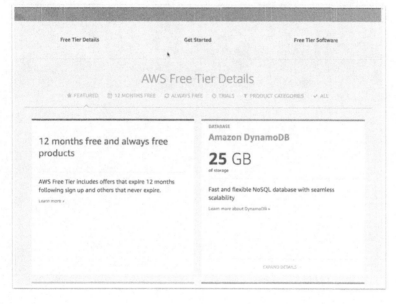

Click on the Free Tier Button to Get Started

After you have reviewed the list of free services, click on the *Create a Free Account* button to begin the registration process.

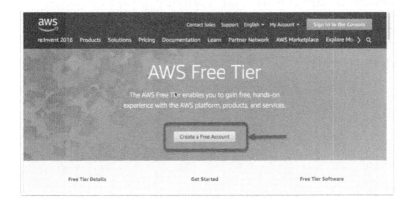

Create Your Login Credentials

Enter your email address and your desired password for your account. You will also have to enter an account name. Click the *Continue* button once you have completed entering this information.

Create an AWS account

AWS Accounts Include
12 Months of Free Tier Access

Including use of Amazon EC2, Amazon S3, and Amazon DynamoDB
Visit **aws.amazon.com/free** for full offer terms

Email address

Password

Confirm password

AWS account name ⓘ

Continue

Sign in to an existing AWS account

© 2019 Amazon Web Services, Inc. or its affiliates.
All rights reserved.
Privacy Policy   Terms of Use

Enter Your Contact Information

Next, enter all of your account information. First, select whether this is a company or personal account. After filling this in, enter the captcha code and then check that you have read the terms and conditions. After completing this, click the *Create Account and Continue* button.

Enter Your Payment Information

Now, enter your credit card information and select the *Continue* button. Even though this is a free account, they still require a credit card number in case you use resources outside the free tier. This account will allow you to use resources outside the free ones, and Amazon does an excellent job of letting you know when you are going to use resources outside the free tier. We will see this in a later chapter, when we create a virtual machine with a free account.

Verify Your Identity

Next, enter your cell phone number for an identity verification check.

Enter Your PIN

Complete the Verification

Next, click the *Continue to select your Support Plan* button.

Select Your Support Plan

Select the Basic support plan, which Amazon includes for free. The other plans are paid support plans you can upgrade to later, if you need them. For just getting started with the platform, the basic plan is all you need to get going.

Complete Your Selection

After selecting the basic plan, click the *Continue* button to move to the next step.

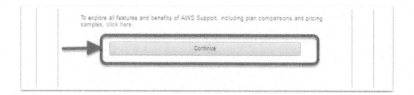

Wait For Your Verification Email

Wait for your verification email. Once you have received this, you can then sign into your account and use AWS. Click the *Sign in to the Console* button to use your new account.

Log Into Your New Account

Enter your email address and password, and then click the *Sign in using our secure server* button to log in.

You Are Now Logged In

Now that you are logged in, you can use AWS services. Click on the ECS icon to get started. We will cover this in more detail in later lessons. Once you are finished using the service, click on the menu, under your name, to log out.

4.3 What is Amazon EC2?

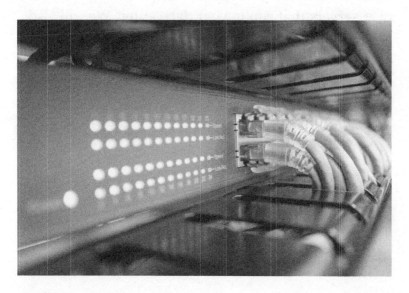

Amazon EC2

Elastic Cloud Compute is AWS's virtualization service. EC2 was released in 2006 and has had many features added since that time. Pricing is based on the size and type of machine you configure. You only pay for what you use. Pricing is by the hour. (Partial hours are billed by what you actually consume) EC2 offers many tools and features, which make it very flexible for managing online servers. EC2 is one of AWS's most popular services.

In this section, we will look at some of the attributes of the EC2 service and some of the advantages it offers over servers that run in your datacenter. We will also look at the cost models that are available for this service.

Advantages of EC2

You can quickly provision new servers to fulfill new demands. (within minutes) This is as opposed to buying and installing physical hardware that might take weeks, or even months, to complete. Also, you can provision servers with software that is already installed. When you order physical hardware, you will have to install and configure software from scratch on a brand new machine.

You can quickly backup machines, while they are running, using snapshots. This is a quick and easy way to recover from unplanned problems. In the traditional model of a datacenter, backups are often done by special purpose software. Restoring from these backup images is often a long and difficult process.

You can easily develop your own custom server images. This is done through a mechanism called AMI. (Amazon Machine Interface) By using this, you can develop custom images that will support your operations. You can use this as a base image with specific software installed on your server. By doing this, you can then deploy new servers with a custom configuration already installed. This will result in a huge saving of labor with future deployments.

You only pay for what you use. Machines that are shut down do not incur runtime charges, only storage costs. Storage costs are really cheap in the cloud. As such, you almost pay nothing for a server that is shut down. Many applications that run in a datacenter are only needed at specific times. For these types of applications, you can turn on the server when you need it and shut it down when not needed. This technique can result in significant savings.

Once machines are no longer needed, you can simply delete them. This allows you to spin up a machine for a special project, and then get rid of them once the project has been completed. If you were doing this with dedicated hardware in your own datacenter, you would be stuck with either finding another use for the computer, or trying to dispose of it somehow.

Cost Model

EC2 supports several cost models for various types of applications.

- On Demand
- Spot Instances
- Savings Plan (Long Term Commitment)
- Dedicated Host

On Demand

The on-demand model is the most expensive of the four models described here. There is no upfront cost or commitment required. You simply pay by the house based on the size of the machine, the configuration, and the regions the machine is located in.

Spot Instances

Next on the list are spot instances. If you have an application that needs to be run periodically and the exact time of the day it runs is not critical . This is a good model for these types of applications. You can run these during off times, where the cost of using the servers is a much lower hourly rate.

Savings Plan (Long Term Commitment)

If you know you will have an application running long term. You can sign a longer term commitment to lower your operating cost. This is a good option for applications that are stable from a resource utilization perspective.

Dedicated Host

This last option is an offering where you can get dedicated hardware for your environment to run applications. This option requires a specified term for the contract.

On Demand Cost Example

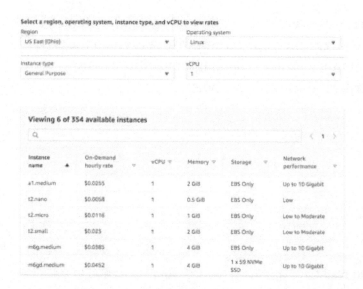

Select a region, operating system, instance type, and vCPU to view rates

Region	Operating system
US East (Ohio)	Linux

Instance type	vCPU
General Purpose	1

Viewing 6 of 354 available instances

Instance name	On-Demand hourly rate	vCPU	Memory	Storage	Network performance
a1.medium	$0.0255	1	2 GiB	EBS Only	Up to 10 Gigabit
t2.nano	$0.0058	1	0.5 GiB	EBS Only	Low
t2.micro	$0.0116	1	1 GiB	EBS Only	Low to Moderate
t2.small	$0.023	1	2 GiB	EBS Only	Low to Moderate
m6g.medium	$0.0385	1	4 GiB	EBS Only	Up to 10 Gigabit
m6gd.medium	$0.0452	1	4 GiB	1 x 59 NVMe SSD	Up to 10 Gigabit

The example above describes the hourly pricing for Linux instances in the Ohio region, based on memory and CPU configurations.
Source: https://aws.amazon.com/ec2/pricing/on-demand/

Migration Tools

There are several migration tools available that can make migrating your on-premise servers to the AWS Cloud much easier. The diagram below briefly describes some of these tools.

Migration Evaluator - tools to plan for migration

AWS Migration Hub - single source location to track migration projects

AWS Prescriptive Guidance - a resource that describes best practices

Amazon Lightsail

Amazon Lightsail

Although this is not part of the EC2 service, it is closely related. Amazon Lightsail is a simplified consumer grade service for virtualization. It offers preconfigured server packages for popular configurations that you can pick from a menu. Lightsail servers have low-cost options that are billed monthly. Packages include network options, such as static IP addresses.

Summary

Amazon EC2 offers a way for organizations to migrate their on-premise servers to the cloud. EC2 is highly flexible and cost effective. It offers the distinct advantage that you only pay for what you use. Amazon Lightsail offers a simplified version of the service for consumer and smaller applications.

4.4 How to Create a Virtual Machine Using Amazon AWS

Now that you have your account with Amazon AWS, I will describe how you can quickly create a virtual server, in the cloud.

Navigate to the AWS Homepage

Go to https://aws.amazon.com. Click the *Sign in to the Console* button to log in. If you would like to view a video of this process on my YouTube channel, click here..

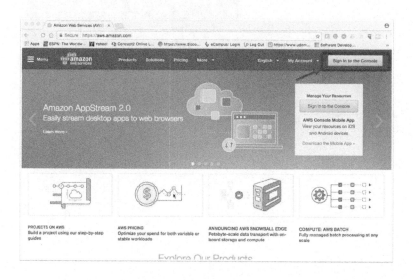

Log into Your Account

Use the username and password you chose to sign up for your account.

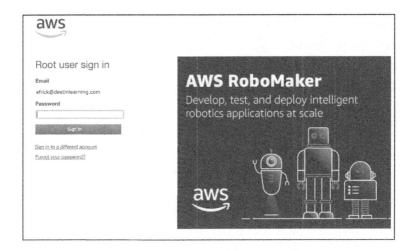

Navigate to the Services Page

Click the Services link in the upper left-hand portion of the screen.

Click the EC2 Link

Once the services are displayed, click the EC2 link to bring up the pages used to manage virtual machines.

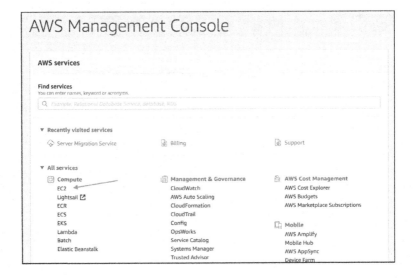

Navigate to the Instances Page

Click the instances link, to the left, to open the EC2 instance manager page. On this page, you will see the list of machines you already have running (if you have any), and you will have the option of creating a new one there.

Click the *Launch Instance* Button

Once this page has opened, you can review the status of any other machine in your account. Here, I already have several virtual machines created. In your case, you will have a brand-new account, and there will be no machines listed. Once this page has loaded, click the *Launch Instance* button.

Select the Instance Image

Scroll through the list and select the instance you would like to create. Here, I will use the Windows Server 2016 Base image. Notice, the instance types that are free tier eligible, have a label indicating that.

Select the Instance Type

This page should default to the t2.micro, which is a small, but free machine to operate. The other types listed are larger machines for which you will incur costs for using. If this computer is not fast enough for your task, you can upgrade later, on the fly. One of the significant advantages of cloud computing is the ease with which you can add resources to your projects. For this exercise, accept the default by clicking the *Review and Launch* button.

Launch your Virtual Machine

At this point, you are ready to launch your new virtual machine. The system will warn you about your security group, and that it could be made to be more secure. Do not worry about this for this exercise, since it is only a development computer. If you want to use this to store more personal data later, I would recommend locking this down at a later time. Click the *Launch* button to continue.

Select the Key Pair for Your Machine

You must have a key to launch a new machine. You can use that key later to retrieve the password. Select *Create a new key pair*, and assign a name for that key. Once you have entered the name, you must download the key and store it on your local computer. You will need this key later, to retrieve the password for your new virtual machine. Click the *Download Key Pair* button.

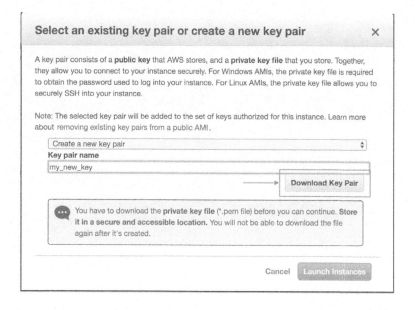

Note Where Your File is Stored

You will need this file later, so look in your browser window to note the file location.

my_new_key.pem
https://console.aws.amazon.com/ec2/v2/downloadKeyPair

Show in Finder

×

Click the Launch Instances Button

Now that you have your key file, click the *Launch Instances* button to begin the build process.

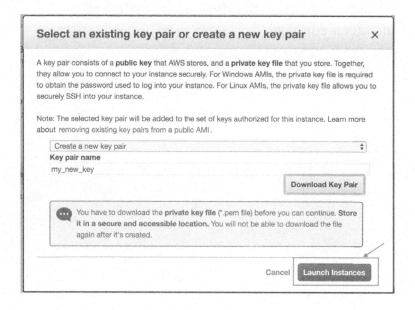

Check the Launch Status

This window will alert you to the status of your new instance. Click the *View Instance* button, at the bottom of the page, to return to the instances management page.

Check Your New Instance Status

When you return to this page, you will see the status of your new server. Once the round indicator turns green, your new machine has been created and is running.

Get the Windows Password

Right-mouse-click on your new server, and select the *Get Windows Password* selection from the menu.

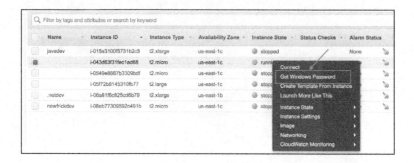

Select the Key File

Once this window comes up, select the *Choose File* button, and then select the key file you created in the previous step.

Open the Key File

Navigate to where you stored your key file, select the
file, and click the *Open* button.

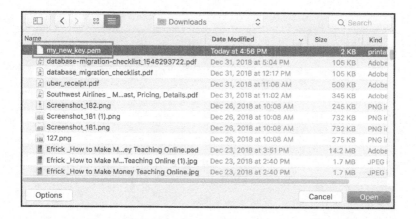

Click the *Decrypt Password* Button

Once the key file has been loaded, click the *Decrypt Password* button to get your Windows system password.

Note Your New Password

The system has assigned a new password to you. You can view this at the bottom of the window. Record this so you can use it in the next step. (You can highlight the password, copy it, and paste it into a text file on your system to make it easier to manage, or you can write it down.) Click the *Close* button when you finish recording your password.

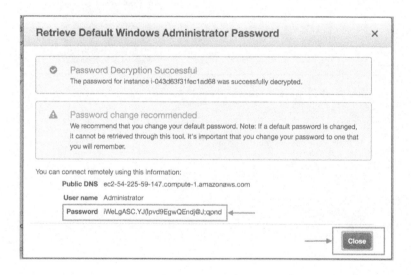

Click the Connect Button

Now that you have your password, you can connect to your running computer. Right-mouse-click on the running computer line and then click the *Connect* link, in the menu.

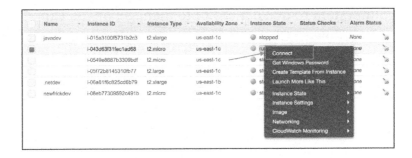

Download the Remote Desktop File

Click the *Download Remote Desktop File* button, so you can use the remote desktop to log into your new computer.

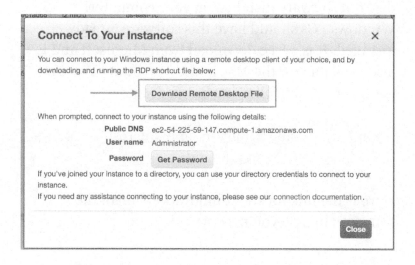

Navigate to the Remote Desktop File

Once the file download completes, open the directory where the file is. Double click on the file to open the remote desktop software. Note, you must have remote desktop software installed on your computer. Windows PCs should have this software already installed. It is a free download from Microsoft and is also available for the Mac in the App Store. You can get this from the following link for Mac:

https://itunes.apple.com/us/app/microsoft-remote-desktop-10/id1295203466?mt=12

Here is the link for the Windows version of the software, in case you need it:

https://www.microsoft.com/en-us/p/microsoft-remote-desktop-preview/9nblggh3oh88?activetab=pivot:overviewtab

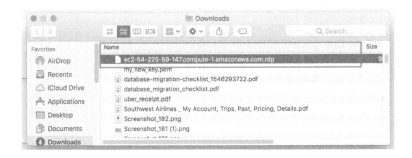

Log Into Your New Machine

Use the password you recorded in the previous step. (It is long and difficult to type in the first time.) After you log in, you can use standard Windows commands to reset the password to something that is easier for you to manage. I recommend pasting the password into a document and then printing it out to log in the first time. The password is complicated to write down correctly.

You Should Now Be Logged In

If all goes well, your computer is running, you should now be logged in, and you can use your computer for anything you want. Even though this is a free tier computer, you only have a limited number of free hours, so shut it down when you are not using it. You can either shut it down from the server, or from the Amazon command line.

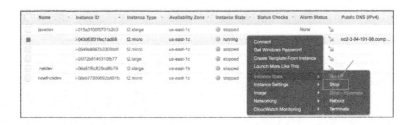

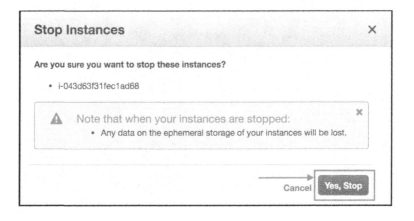

4.5 What is Amazon S3?

Amazon S3

In this section, we will review Amazon's S3 storage service. S3 stands for Simple Cloud Storage Service and is one of AWS oldest services. AWS launched S3 in 2006.

S3 is designed for very high durability (S3 is designed for 99.999999999%) (11 9s) This means, in practice, you will never lose any data in S3.

It is a flexible service and it is very easy to use. Many companies that are migrating to the cloud choose this as one of their first migration points, since it is straightforward to use and cost effective.

In the next few pages, we will explore more details of the S3 service.

S3 Benefits

The AWS S3 service was one of the first services that Amazon offered on the platform. This storage service offers many advantages. Some of these include:

- Easy to scale for massive amounts of storage
- A large number of storage classes to support many different usage scenarios
- Can be easily configured to replicate data to multiple regions
- Easy to configure for data flow scenarios and archiving
- Programmatic access to support online systems and processing

Common Use Cases

Due to the flexibility and features included in S3, it can support a wide variety of use cases for storage applications. Some of these include:

- Backup and Restore
- Disaster Recovery
- Archiving
- Data lakes and big data analytics
- Hybrid cloud storage
- Cloud-native applications
- Hosting static websites

Detailed Use Case

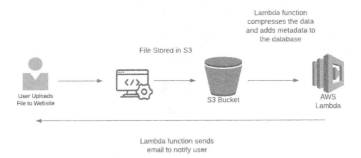

The use case above describes a typical scenario in which S3 can interact with other services. In this scenario, a user uploads a file to a website. From there, it is stored in an S3 bucket. Once it is uploaded to S3, a Lambda function is triggered that compresses the file and tags it with metadata. When this function has completed, it sends an email notification back to the user.

S3 has a ton of features that are well beyond the scope of this book. The thing to take away from this chapter is that S3 is a very easy to use, flexible, and durable cloud-based storage system.

S3 Storage Classes

Storage Class	Description
S3 Standard	Designed for frequently
S3 Intelligent-Tiering	Designed for automatic cost
S3 Standard-1A	For data that is less
S3 Standard Zone 1A	For data that is less
S3 Glacier	Low-cost storage class for
S3 Glacier Deep Archive	S3's lowest-cost storage

Summary

Amazon S3 is a complete cloud storage solution. It offers low cost and high performance. Multiple storage classes are available to support different use cases. APIs are available to access S3 from other services. This helps facilitate many end-to-end solutions.

4.6 Deploying a Website on Amazon S3

In this section, I will show you how to deploy a website on Amazon S3. There are several advantages of hosting websites on Amazon S3. These advantages include:

- It is simple to use.
- It is very inexpensive to use for hosting.
- You can easily integrate with CloudFront.
- This process can easily be automated via scripts.

In the next few pages, I will cover the step-by-step details of how you can host a simple website.

How to Build a Simple Website with Amazon S3

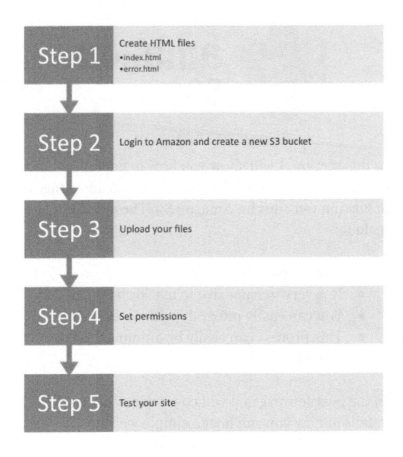

Step 1 — Create HTML files
- index.html
- error.html

Step 2 — Login to Amazon and create a new S3 bucket

Step 3 — Upload your files

Step 4 — Set permissions

Step 5 — Test your site

Step 1 Sample HTML Files

The following are listings of two sample HTML files we can use for building the world's simplest website on Amazon S3. You can use any files you wish, I used these for simplicity.

index.html

```html
<html>

<h1>This is our test website for Amazon
S3</h1>

        <p> Hello World!</p>

</html>
```

error.html

```html
<html>
<h1>OOPS an error has occurred!</h1>

    <p> This is our test S3 website.</p>

</html>
```

Step 2 Create an S3 bucket

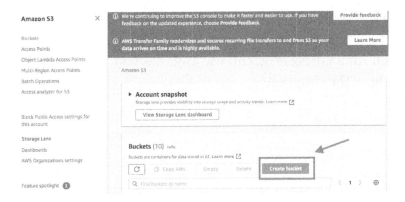

First, navigate to the S3 service page in AWS. Once you are there, click on the *Create Bucket* button that I indicated above.

Step 2 continued

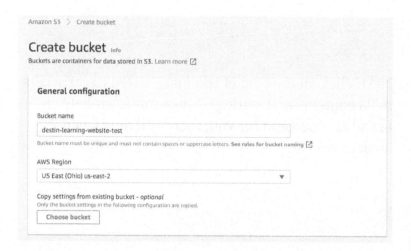

Select a name for your bucket, as in the following screenshot. Please note that the name for your bucket must be unique. Uncheck the **Block *all* public access selection.** Also, check **I acknowledge that the current settings might result in this bucket and the objects within becoming public.**

Once you have completed this, click the *Create Bucket* button.

Step 2 continued

	destin-learning-website-test	US East (Ohio) us-east-2	Objects can be public	October 16, 2021, 15:29:47 (UTC-04:00)

Next, click on the bucket you just created to get access to its contents and settings. Since this is probably a brand new account for you, there will only be one buck in the list.

Step 3 Upload Your Files

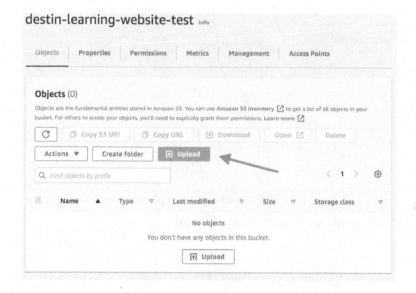

After you have opened your bucket, you will see the following screen. Click on the *Upload* button to upload your two HTML files.

Step 3 Upload Your Files - continued

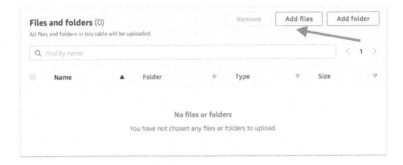

Click on the *Add Files* button to upload the two html files. (index.html and error.html)

Step 3 Upload Your Files - continued

You should now see the files listed in your S3 bucket. Next, click the *Close* button to return to the bucket summary screen.

Step 4 Set Permissions

Under the properties tab, scroll down to the bottom of
the page and edit the Static website hosting settings.

Static website hosting
Use this bucket to host a website or redirect requests. Learn more

Static website hosting
Disabled

Edit

Step 4 Set Permissions - continued

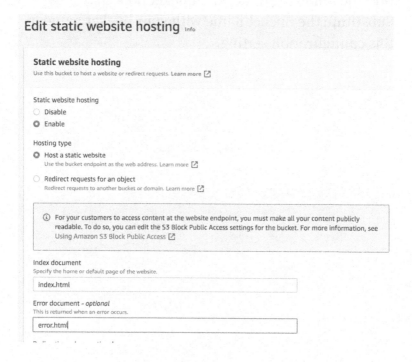

Enter in the file names for index and error files, and then click the *Save changes* button.

Step 4 Set Permissions - continued

Add the following under the Bucket policies.
Substitute the bucket name with your bucket name in
this configuration setting.

```
{
    "Version":"2012-10-17",
    "Statement":[{
      "Sid":"PublicReadGetObject",
      "Effect":"Allow",
      "Principal": "*",
      "Action":["s3:GetObject"],
      "Resource":["arn:aws:s3:::destin-learning-
website-test/*"]
    }]
  }
```

Step 5 Test Your Website

Click on the URL displayed at the bottom of the Static website hosting section, and you should see your new website. You should now see the following in your browser.

This is our test website for Amazon S3

Hello World!

Summary

I have shown you how simple it is to set up a website using Amazon S3. Although these were simple HTML files, you could replace these with any HTML files and your website will instantly be live worldwide. Try playing around with this to see what you can create.

Chapter 5 Cloud Career Information

In this chapter, I have included some brief information about careers in cloud computing. In the first section, I have included some information from a recent survey about the top cloud jobs and associated salary information. Following that, I have included some information about the top cloud certifications that are in demand in the market today.

5.1 Top Cloud Jobs and Salaries

The cloud computing market continues to grow at an amazing rate. The demand for trained cloud personnel remains strong and currently there is a shortage of trained personnel. To give you an idea of the top jobs that are in demand, I have included some data from Randstad Research that lists some of the most in-demand cloud jobs for 2021.

Cloud Job	Average Salary
Cloud engineers	$132,866 USD
DevOps developers	$137,830 USD
.NET developers	$131,070 USD
Machine-learning	$137,513 USD
Security analysts	$124,892 USD

I have included the link to the Randstadt site below if you would like to see further details:

https://www.randstadusa.com/job-seeker/best-jobs/best-jobs-tech/#cloud_engineer

5.2 Top Cloud Certifications

In this section, I will cover the top cloud certification in the market today. With the shortage of trained cloud personnel, certifications have become much more important in the marketplace than they were five to ten years ago. Now it is much more common to land a cloud-related job with only cloud certifications and no formal IT college degree. This was not the case in the market five to ten years prior, when many companies required a computer science degree or equivalent.

This market shift has also created an explosion in the IT training market, particularly with online IT training companies. The cloud providers themselves are also offering training to help fill the shortage of trained cloud engineers. Amazon, Microsoft and

Google all offer a wide variety of certifications to cover various aspects of their platforms.

The following list is a list that Global Knowledge created based on a survey they did in 2020 of IT Skills and Salary. You should note that the list includes certifications from all three major cloud providers and some cloud neutral certifications as well.

Rank	Certification
1	AWS Certified Solutions Architect –
2	Microsoft Certified: Azure Administr
3	Google Certified Professional Cloud
4	AWS Certified Developer – Associate
5	Google Certified Professional Data E
6	Microsoft Certified: Microsoft Azure
7	AWS Certified SysOps Administrator
8	CCSP – Certified Cloud Security Prof
9	CompTIA Cloud+
10	Microsoft Certified: Azure Solutions

Chapter 6 Summary

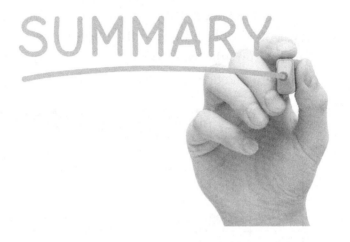

In this chapter I will wrap up the material for this book. I will present a brief summary of the course and then follow up with some more detailed information about me and how you can contact me if you are interested. I have also included some links to my additional publications as well as some additional material on my YouTube channel.

6.1 Course Summary

Thank you so much for reading this book. I hope it has given you a good start on your journey to learn more about computer science and cloud computing. As I mentioned in the introduction, this book is part of a series of books designed to train entry-level software developers. If you have suggestions for improvements for this book, please contact me, as I would love to hear from you. Also, please leave a review for me, so I can continually make this book better. Thank you again, and I hope to see you again soon.

6.2 About the Author

Eric Frick

I have worked in software development and IT operations for 30 years. I have worked as a Software Developer, Software Development Manager, Software Architect, and as an Operations Manager. Also, for the last five years, I have taught evening classes on various IT related subjects at several local universities. I currently work as a Cloud Instructor for Mirantis Inc. (https://mirantis.com), developing cloud-based certification courses. In 2015, I founded destinlearning.com, and I am developing a series of books that can provide practical information to students on various IT and software development topics.

If you would like to connect with me on LinkedIn, here is the link to my profile:
https://www.linkedin.com/in/efrick/

Also, if you have any questions or comments about this book you can contact me directly at:
sales@destinlearning.com

6.3 More From Destin Learning

Thank you so much for your interest in this book. I hope it has given you a good start in the exciting field of Information Technology. If you would like to learn more about software development, you can check out my book, The Beginner's Guide to C#. You can learn more by clicking on the link below.

https://www.destinlearning.com

6.4 Destin Learning YouTube Channel

You can see more on my YouTube channel, where I am continuing to post free videos about software development and information technology. If you subscribe to my channel, you will get updates as I post new material weekly.

https://youtube.com/destinlearning

Appendix

A.1 Cloud Concepts Quiz Answers

1. C
2. C
3. B
4. A
5. C
6. B
7. C
8. B
9. D

Made in the USA
Las Vegas, NV
27 October 2024